IMAGES
of America

CHICAGO'S
LOST "L"S

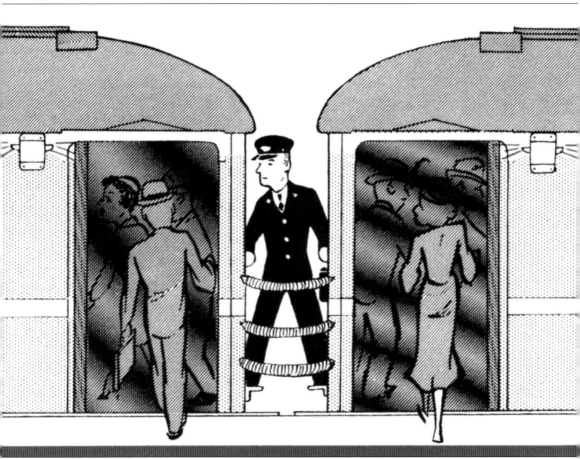

Before 1950, there were no "married pairs" of "L" cars in Chicago. Trains could be as small as a single car. A three-car train required two conductors whose jobs were to open the passenger entry doors (which were on the sides at the ends of the cars) using controls situated between the cars. To operate his side doors, a conductor had to stand between the cars—in any weather. Conductors told the motorman when to proceed and had to observe when the doors were clear. A bell system was used to notify the motorman. Two dings meant "proceed," and one ding meant "hold." The rearmost conductor started with his bell, then the next rearmost, and so on, until two dings rang in the motorman's compartment, which was his signal to go. The longer the train, the longer it took to leave the station. The New York elevated had multiple unit door controls in the 1920s, but after the Depression, the Chicago "L" lacked money to install them, even though it would have saved on labor costs. (Author's collection.)

ON THE COVER: In this 1950 photograph, Chicago Transit Authority motormen and conductors prepare to depart the Ravenswood "L" terminal at Kimball and Lawrence Avenues in the Albany Park neighborhood on Chicago's northwest side. "L" car No. 392 was built in 1905 by the American Car & Foundry Company for the South Side "L." It was retired in 1957. (Author's collection.)

IMAGES
of America

CHICAGO'S
LOST "L"S

David Sadowski

ARCADIA
PUBLISHING

Published by Arcadia Publishing
Charleston, South Carolina

Printed in the United States of America

Library of Congress Control Number: 2020947748

For all general information, please contact Arcadia Publishing:
Telephone 843-853-2070
Fax 843-853-0044
E-mail sales@arcadiapublishing.com
For customer service and orders:
Toll-Free 1-888-313-2665

Visit us on the Internet at www.arcadiapublishing.com

To Raymond DeGroote Jr., the dean of Chicago railfans

CONTENTS

ACKNOWLEDGMENTS

The author wishes to thank the following individuals, without whose assistance this book would not have been possible: Jack Bejna, Craig Berndt, Glen Brewer, Eric Bronsky, Leslie Engelberg, Graham Garfield, Ross Harano, David Harrison, the late John Horachek, Diana L. Koester, Andre Kristopans, Bruce C. Nelson, Don Ross, J.J. Sedelmaier, William Shapotkin, John Smatlak, David Stanley, George Trapp, and the late Jeffrey L. Wien. Special thanks go out to my editors Stacia Bannerman and Ryan Vied, who helped make this a better book.

The references used in the course of completing this work include:

"Chicago's Metropolitan Elevated Railway." *Leslie's Weekly*. June 6, 1895: 386.

Dana, William B., ed. *Street Railway Supplement of the Commercial & Financial Chronicle, March 9, 1895*. New York: William B. Dana Company, 1895.

Davies, Owen, ed. *Chicago Elevated Railroads Consolidation of Operations, 1913* (reprint). Chicago: Owen Davies, 1967.

"Mass Transportation in Chicago Moves Forward." *Mass Transportation*. January 1939: 5–10.

"Running on the 'L.'" *Chicago Daily Tribune*. June 7, 1892: 9.

"The West Side Metropolitan Elevated Railway System of Chicago." *Scientific American*. April 27, 1895: 264.

For further reading, check out the author's transit blog at www.thetrolleydodger.com.

Unless otherwise noted, all images are from the author's collection.

Note: Chicago's street numbering system, which has been in use since the early 1900s, is in the form of a grid, with State Street being the east–west coordinate and Madison Street the north–south. The numbers provided in parentheses after many of the street names will help readers orient themselves to various locations. For example, there are eight blocks in a mile throughout most of the city, so Western Avenue, which is three miles west of State Street, is written as "2400 W."

INTRODUCTION

Chicago became the fastest growing city in the world as it rose from the ashes of the disastrous 1871 fire. It quickly grew to a size where public transit became a necessity. First came the omnibus, horsecar, cable car, and—finally—the electric streetcar. The streets were congested, and gridlock ensued, especially downtown. New York inventors came up with the idea of elevated railways that would defeat traffic by rising above it. Starting in 1868, the New York El gradually caught on, and by the 1880s, there were several lines in Manhattan. Chicago began to take notice. Elevated railways were no fly-by-night undertaking. They required major capital and held the promise of major profits.

Numerous companies were formed to construct elevated railways in Chicago, but only four succeeded—the South Side Rapid Transit Railroad Company (1892), Lake Street Elevated Railroad (1893), Metropolitan West Side Elevated (1895), and Northwestern Elevated Railroad (1900). Chicago's south side was more developed than the north and west sides (there is only a small east side, far to the south due to the shape of Lake Michigan), and that is where the first "L" (as Chicagoans refer to it) was built.

When Chicago was chosen by Congress to host the World's Columbian Exposition in 1890, the city had to get serious with building the "L"s in a hurry. The 1893 world's fair also spurred a grade-separation movement in Chicago. Many existing railroads were put on embankments between 1890 and 1910. The "L"s were part of that movement. The South Side "L" began service on June 6, 1892, and was an immediate success. It was colloquially known as the Alley "L," since its original route to Thirty-ninth Street ran next to an alleyway, even though it was built on private property. Like the New York "L"s, it used small steam engines to pull unpowered coaches. The "L" was extended to Jackson Park, site of the world's fair, the following year. At the exposition, visitors were transported by the experimental Columbian Intramural Railway, which was powered by electricity. By the end of 1893, the Lake Street "L" had started running to the west side. Soon, service reached as far west as suburban Oak Park, again powered by steam.

The Metropolitan West Side Elevated opened on May 6, 1895, and was innovative in several respects. First, it used electricity from the start. Second, it was planned with several branch lines, and third, it had four tracks near the downtown area, facilitating express trains in addition to locals. Fourth, it had adequate yards and shops, mostly at the ends of lines. These were important advantages over the other "L"s, which eventually were retrofitted with a third track for express trains over parts of their lines; at times, it was difficult to find adequate storage space for trains. All three "L"s suffered from the same problem—inadequate distribution downtown. Their stub-end terminals were all located on the outskirts and therefore limited their appeal. High start-up costs led to bankruptcies, reorganizations, and corporate name changes.

Enter Charles Tyson Yerkes (1837–1905), often called the "Robber Baron" of Chicago transit. Yerkes controlled several street railways on the north and west sides. He saw the new "L"s as both a threat and an opportunity, and he seized the moment. First, he took over the Lake Street "L." Next, he had a brilliant idea—a downtown "Union Loop" (known as "the Loop") that would solve the distribution problem faced by all the "L"s. They would all benefit, but obtaining the necessary permissions from businesses and the city was a complex and difficult undertaking. Fortunately, Yerkes was up to the task. The Lake Street "L" line was extended east to Wabash Avenue, putting one fourth of the Loop in place. Once it had this advantage, the South Side "L" pressed for an extension, which became the Wabash leg in 1896.

Yerkes formed a new railroad just to build the Van Buren Street and Fifth Avenue (now Wells Street) legs—a railroad that never intended to run any trains but would simply collect 10 percent of each ticket sold on the Loop, which the "L"s were only too glad to pay. Everyone benefitted when the Union Loop was completed and opened on October 3, 1897. Chicago's downtown area would be known as the Loop from that time forward. Ridership on some lines increased by 50 percent once the Loop opened, but tremendous success created congestion. Longer trains with longer platforms were needed, but only so many trains at a time could fit, and trains had to be kept apart for safety. By 1898, steam power was gone, replaced by 600 volts of direct current coursing through a third rail. Inventor Frank Julian Sprague (1857–1934) was tapped to convert the South Side "L" to electricity, and he did so with his latest invention, multiple unit control. Instead of having one engine pulling unpowered trailers, each car had motors that were controlled by the head car and acted in unison. It was a much better system and was soon in wide use.

The most notable quote attributed to Yerkes is not something he actually said. He did not say, "It's the straphangers that pay the dividends." Crowded trains were more profitable, but when things get too crowded, a company would start losing riders and have a lot of angry customers. What Yerkes did say at a stockholders' meeting was that a short-haul rider was more profitable than a long-haul one, since both paid the same fare. That is simple mathematics, but it explains the problem that the "L" eventually faced—it had a lot of long-haul riders that cost more to carry, limiting potential profits. The "L" started with a nickel fare, but raising it would prove difficult because politics were involved. Riders wanted fast and frequent reliable service, but they also wanted low fares. Yerkes's final major contribution was the Northwestern Elevated Railroad, which gave the north side its first "L" on May 31, 1900. The city limited the Northwestern to two tracks south of Chicago Avenue (800 N.), but there were four tracks from there to the end of the line at Wilson Avenue (4600 N.). A year after the Northwestern "L" opened, Yerkes cashed out his local interests and moved to England, where he was instrumental in organizing the London Underground. He died a few years later.

In the early 1900s, all four "L"s worked to extend service by building branch lines—a boon to development. The only downside was that new lines meant more Loop trains and riders, which made the congestion problem worse. Now that the four companies had to cooperate, the idea of combining them became more attractive. Yerkes's interests in the Lake Street and Northwestern "L"s meant they worked together well. After he was gone, it was left to Samuel Insull (1859–1938) to bring it all together. Electric railways were major customers for Insull's Commonwealth Edison. They also helped spread electric power to outlying areas where, in some cases, individuals bought their home electricity from the local interurban, which had the infrastructure.

If not for the Union Loop, Chicago's future might have turned out more like Boston's, where the Red, Green, Orange, and Blue Lines all have different equipment and are incompatible on each other's tracks. While Chicago avoided this fate, there were still enough differences that it has only been since the early 2000s that all "L" trains could run on all the lines. Insull's first move, after taking control of the four firms, was the formation of the Chicago Elevated Railways Collateral Trust. Technically, there were still four separate companies, but starting in 1913, they would operate as a unit. Loop operations were reorganized, and the north- and south-side lines were through-routed. Previously, all trains either went around the Loop or to one of four stub-end terminals. Now, many north- and south-side trains would go to the other side of town, travelling on only half of the Loop, increasing the number of trains that could run there. The Loop, which had been bidirectional, would now run counterclockwise on inner and outer tracks. This system remained in effect until 1969. Finally, riders could transfer between "L" lines without paying an additional fare. Transfer bridges were put up at Loop stations. A transfer station was built where the Met crossed over the Lake Street "L."

Until 1913, all "L" cars were made of wood and steel. From 1913 forward, they were all steel, and over the next decade, the "L" got 455 new state-of-the-art cars (the 4000-series). By 1924, the four "L" companies had merged into the Chicago Rapid Transit Company. By then, Insull also controlled all three major Chicago interurbans: the North Shore Line, South Shore Line, and the Chicago, Aurora & Elgin Railroad. Two of these ran into the city by "L." It was possible to board a fast train on the Loop and take it 90 miles north to Milwaukee, Wisconsin, or go to Aurora or Elgin. After numerous line extensions, the privately owned "L" system reached its maximum length in 1930. Many extensions were made at ground level in outlying areas, and some of these lines used overhead wire for at least part of the time instead of third rail.

When it was convenient to do so, new service was often started under a lease arrangement with another railroad. The most important such extension took place in 1908. The Chicago, Milwaukee, St. Paul & Pacific Railroad (known as the Milwaukee Road) no longer wanted to operate its steam commuter service on one of its north side lines. The Northwestern took this over, and with modifications, it became the Evanston Extension. By 1912, it went to Wilmette.

Insull improved the North Shore Line via the new Skokie Valley Route, which connected to the "L" at Howard Street. A new "L" branch went to Niles Center in 1925. The following year, the Met's Garfield Park "L" was extended to Bellwood and Westchester on tracks owned by the Chicago, Aurora & Elgin. This was meant to be part of a similar bypass route for that interurban.

As successful as they were, elevated railroads became controversial in major cities as they were considered urban blight. In New York, the city government wanted to tear down all the elevated lines in Manhattan and replace them with expensive subways.

Municipal ownership became another hot-button issue. Cities were always heavily invested in transit issues but often clashed with private operators who were trying to make a profit while serving the public. Fares were kept artificially low, lines were heavily regulated, and the process of changing or abandoning service was often difficult. Chicago wanted half-fare rates for children and free transfers between the "L" and the Surface Lines, which was competition to some extent; these reduced both revenues and profits.

In New York City in the 1920s, Mayor John Hylan became such an adversary of the two rapid transit firms that he wanted the city to compete with them. This resulted in the creation of the Independent (IND) Subway, which entered service in 1932. It undermined the IRT and BMT to such an extent that the city bought them out less than 10 years later. However, the cost of building the IND Subway nearly bankrupted the city.

The 1920s were boom years for Chicago and its transit. Population and ridership increased greatly. But all this came to a crashing end with the Great Depression. The Insull empire was a victim of this crash in 1932. Ridership and revenues plummeted, and the Chicago Rapid Transit Company—plus the three interurbans—went into bankruptcy. The City of Chicago wanted subways, but private companies could not build them. They were expensive. The city also wanted to merge the Rapid Transit and Surface Lines companies, and various failed attempts were made to force them into a shotgun marriage. Chicago did not want municipal ownership, fearing a repeat of what happened in New York. The growth years were over for the "L." Now, the Chicago Rapid Transit Company was barely able to keep going and had no money to buy new equipment. The "L" only accounted for one-sixth of local transit ridership. Very little happened for 15 years, except that facilities and equipment got older. Chicago mayor Ed Kelly, an ally of Pres. Franklin D. Roosevelt, sought federal aid to help build the city's first subway and put people back to work. Secretary of the Interior Harold Ickes studied the plans, modified them, and offered them to the city on a take-it-or-leave-it basis; the city agreed to them. Ickes and the city also wanted to use the subway to bring about transit unification in Chicago. The first subway opened in 1943, about the time the city gave up on the dream of a Chicago Transit Company. Instead, it got the Chicago Transit Authority (CTA), a semi-independent government body with no taxing authority.

The CTA took over the streetcar and "L" companies on October 1, 1947, and began moving quickly to modernize and rationalize the combined system. Streetcars had to compete for space with cars and trucks, which gave the "L" an advantage. But while Chicago had some express trains, it did not really have a true express service. Some lines had stations as close as two blocks away from one another. The goal of the CTA was to put the "rapid" back into rapid transit. Many changes were made, and for various reasons, some of the "L" branches were pruned from the tree. Thus, the Garfield Park, Humboldt Park, Kenwood, Normal Park, Niles Center, Stock Yards, and Westchester "L"s fell by the wayside, along with the outer portion of Douglas Park.

The stories behind how this came to be are almost like a secret history of Chicago itself. The "L" is the backbone of the city. Hop aboard, the doors will soon be closing—please step inside while we tell the tale of *Chicago's Lost "L"s.*

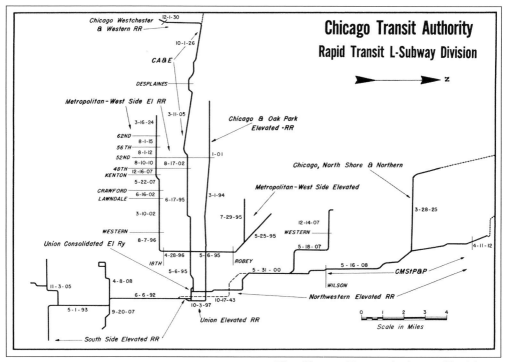

Chicago Transit Authority
Rapid Transit L-Subway Division

MAP OF THE
CHICAGO ELEVATED RAILWAYS
SYSTEM

The Chicago Transit Authority (CTA) took over the "L" system, as shown here, on October 1, 1947. This map shows when various lines opened. Some dates are approximate. Parts of the system were leased, and the names of the companies that owned or built various segments are listed. The dotted line is the State Street Subway built by the City of Chicago. The Dearborn-Milwaukee Subway, which opened in 1951, is not shown.

This map, from *Electric Railways*, January 1917 (page 28), shows the Chicago "L" after 25 years. There were a few later extensions, most at ground level. The Northwestern was already raising tracks between Wilson Avenue and Howard Street—a project finished in 1922. The north portion of Evanston was elevated by 1931. The "L" reached its peak under private ownership in 1930, when Westchester was extended.

One

THE SOUTH SIDE "L"

By 1913, the South Side "L" reached its fullest extent, with five branches—Jackson Park, Englewood, Normal Park, Kenwood, and Stock Yards. Only the first two still exist. The Englewood "L" was extended two blocks in 1969 to improve bus transfers. Jackson Park was cut back twice in the 1980s and 1990s and now ends at Cottage Grove Avenue. Several stations were closed over the years, but two (Roosevelt Road and Cermak Road) have returned.

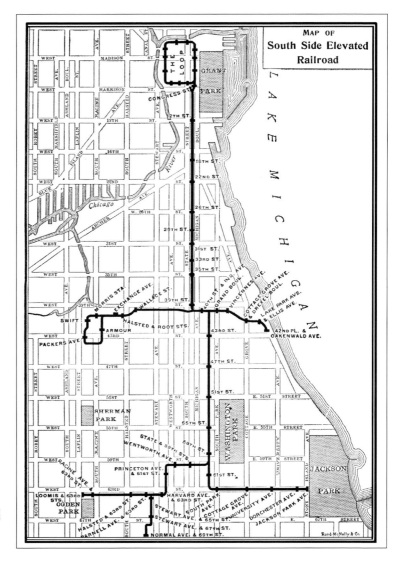

This 1893 South Side "L" train is headed southbound at Twenty-second Street. The Forney-type steam engine is running "tender forward," since there was no way to turn it around downtown. This "L" converted from steam to electricity in 1898. The station was replaced in 1907, when a third track was added between Twelfth and Forty-third Streets. This third track was mostly built over existing alleyways, with stations moved to mezzanine level to provide clearance for alley traffic. The second station closed in 1977, and a new, larger one opened in 2015. Twenty-second Street was renamed Cermak Road after the assassination of Mayor Anton Cermak in 1933.

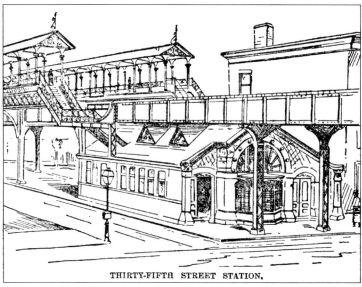

THIRTY-FIFTH STREET STATION.

The *Chicago Tribune's* June 7, 1892, story on the inauguration of service on the South Side "L" included this illustration of the station at Thirty-fifth Street, one of 10 on the line. Service ended at Thirty-ninth Street (the city limits) when the "L's" franchise was approved.

A southbound "L" train approaches the Pershing Road (Thirty-ninth Street) station in April 1941, while children from a local tenement play underneath. This area was the south end of the Bronzeville neighborhood, a center of business and culture in Chicago's African American community. The three-track 'L' ascended here to cross over another nearby railroad. (Russell Lee photograph for the Farm Security Administration.)

The South Side "L" runs east-west at Fortieth Street, where the Kenwood and Stock Yards branches once began. This was a busy location, with lots of riders transferring to other trains, and it had a complex track layout. This photograph is looking west at Indiana Avenue, while Kenwood was a through line. The center-door steel car is a Loop-bound Kenwood train at the junction with the main South Side "L." The four-car train is a north–south through train. The wood train about to cross in front of the Kenwood train is probably a Loop-bound Englewood train. The Chicago Junction Railway freight tracks are at right.

This three-car CTA Howard Express, made up of 4000-series "L" cars, started on the Jackson Park branch. The rearmost car (No. 4057) was older than the other two; it was built in 1914 and retired in 1964. This picture was taken looking west at Indiana Avenue (at Fortieth Street) in June 1949. On August 1, 1949, the CTA replaced express and local service on the north–south lines with A/B skip-stop service, which had proven successful on the Lake Street "L." (L.L. Bonney photograph.)

Everyday people are out and about at the Fifty-eighth Street station on the South Side "L" in this 1946 image. The station house, designed by architect Myron H. Church in the Queen Anne style, was built for the Jackson Park extension, which opened in January 1893. Fifty-eighth Street was an important transfer point between the Jackson Park and Englewood branches. By 1993, Fifty-eighth Street was part of the CTA Green Line, comprising the Lake, Jackson Park, and Englewood lines. This station closed in 1994 and was demolished. (Chicago Transit Authority Historical Collection.)

Garfield Boulevard (formerly Fifty-fifth Street), shown here on July 12, 2013, has the last remaining original station house on the South Side "L," across the street from the current station. Garfield station opened on October 1, 1892, as part of the Jackson Park extension to serve the 1893 World's Columbian Exposition. It remained in use until a new station opened in 2001. Note the distinctive bay and half-cone roof projecting from the building.

The South Side "L" is shown crossing Garfield Boulevard in this 1920s image. Garfield Boulevard is part of a ring of streets that go through parks in the city. When the "L" was built in the early 1890s, park commissioners insisted on decorative support columns where it crossed this boulevard—a feature that remains today.

The Harvard "L" station on the Englewood branch, at 303 West Sixty-third Street, opened in November 1906. Starting in 1907, this is also where trains from the short Normal Park branch originated. This picture was taken around 1908. The Harvard station closed in 1992 and was demolished soon after.

The Englewood "L" runs east-west just south of Sixty-third Street. Englewood had two steam train stations—Englewood Union Station and this one, commonly known as Little Englewood Station, at Sixty-third Street and Wallace Streets, which was once served by the Erie, Monon, Wabash, Chicago & Eastern Illinois and Chicago & Western Indiana Railroads. Metra Southwest Service commuter trains still use these tracks but do not stop here. The Balaban and Katz Southtown Theatre, at 610 West Sixty-third Street, seated 3,201 and opened on December 25, 1931, as the final great Chicago movie palace. It closed in 1958 and was demolished in 1991. This picture was taken in August 1966, and there are CTA 6000s overhead.

The "L" and streetcar lines were competitors; both relied on foot traffic from densely populated neighborhoods. Even in the pre-CTA era, there were places where convenient transfers could be made, such as the Englewood "L" station at Sixty-third and Halsted Streets. This July 4, 1949, photograph is looking east. Chicago Surface Lines car No. 2802 is on a charter trip. Until 1927, riders could change here for Chicago and Interurban Traction trolleys to Kankakee. Once the Illinois Central electrified in 1926 and elevated its tracks, the interurban could not compete and was abandoned. Buses operated by South Suburban Safeway and Suburban Transit also began their runs here.

The Jackson Park "L" crosses a former Illinois Central (now Metra) commuter line at Sixty-third Street. This pre-1913 picture shows the old Woodlawn station before electrification. The Illinois Central used steam until 1926. In 1982, the "L" bridge was closed because of structural defects, and it was not replaced. The east portion of Jackson Park "L" was truncated first to University Avenue, then Cottage Grove.

Stony Island (1600 E.) became the east terminal of the Jackson Park "L" once the World's Columbian Exposition closed in 1893. During the fair, the "L" continued about a block east of here. Stony Island was an important transfer point, served by Sixty-third Street streetcars and Greyhound buses, as shown in this picture taken on November 29, 1951. The line has since been cut back to Cottage Grove. (Truman Hefner photograph.)

Chicago Rapid Transit Company "L" car No. 328 is signed as a Stock Yards local at Indiana Avenue in this September 1936 photograph. The Stock Yards line was a shuttle, originating at this station. Car No. 328 was built by American Car and Foundry in 1905. The Stock Yards line featured a single-track loop and thus did not really have an "end of the line." A small yard was built along the line but quickly removed, as it was unnecessary. The express track was used for midday car storage, as shown here.

This picture taken on May 21, 1934, shows how the CRT Stock Yards "L" branch was extensively damaged by fire two days earlier in a blaze that also destroyed part of the Union Stock Yards; it was said to be the largest conflagration in Chicago since the Great Chicago Fire in 1871. Service west of Halsted Street did not resume until January 16, 1935.

This 1949 image is looking east from the Exchange Avenue station on the Stock Yards branch.

This is the Stock Yards "L," looking east toward the Exchange Avenue station, on June 7, 1927.

The CTA Stock Yards line is pictured looking east from the Exchange station in September 1957, shortly before it was abandoned. Little of what is shown here still exists today except for the shuttered Stock Yards National Bank Building at 4146 South Halsted Street, whose clock tower is at right.

This view is looking east at the Racine Avenue station, the first station Stock Yards trains arrived at when entering the single-track loop. There were four stations: Racine (its original name was Morris), Swift, Packers, and Armour, and trains ran around this loop in a counterclockwise direction. The returning single track merged with this one on the right side, immediately behind the truss bridge seen here.

This view is looking east along the single-track section of the Stock Yards loop at Exhange Avenue and Packers Avenue. The Racine Avenue station is off in the distance. This train is turning south toward the Swift station. Stations on this loop had but one platform.

The remnants of the Swift and Company station on the Stock Yards branch are pictured about one year after CTA service ended on October 7, 1957. Much of the structure had already been removed, except over the Chicago Junction Railway (CJR) freight tracks. CJR owned the Stock Yards and Kenwood "L" branches and leased them to the rapid transit companies between 1907 and 1957. (Charles L. Tauscher photograph.)

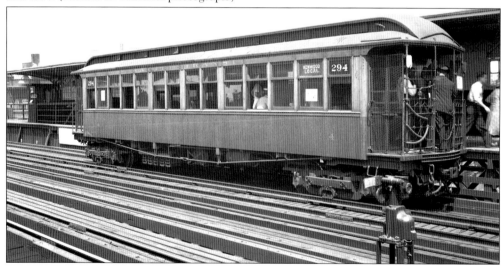

CRT car No. 294 is signed as a Kenwood Local on July 21, 1934. When this photograph was taken, Kenwood ran from Forty-second Place through Indiana Avenue and up to Wilson Avenue on the north side. As with the Jackson Park and Englewood branches, it had both expresses and locals. In 1949, Kenwood became a shuttle ending at Indiana Avenue. The inbound station platform was extended over the northernmost track, and main line north–south service began using the middle track heading downtown.

The Kenwood "L" is shown near the end of service in this 1957 photograph looking east from the end of the Vincennes platform. A third track at left, hidden by the weeds, was used by the Chicago Junction Railway freight line and had a connection to the Illinois Central near the lakefront. (William C. Hoffman photograph.)

The Kenwood "L" was built by the Chicago Junction Railway and rented to the South Side "L." There were five stations between Indiana Avenue and the terminal at Forty-second Place and Oakenwald Avenue, each on an embankment, with a spartan design similar to the one shown in this 1911 view of the Drexel-Cottage Grove station, which had two entrances. (Chicago Transit Authority Historical Collection.)

In this picture from the early 1950s, a Kenwood train is turning west near the lakeshore. At left is Oakenwald Grammar School (at 4071 South Lake Park Avenue), which is now demolished. Most of the Kenwood line ran parallel to Fortieth Street. (William C. Hoffman photograph.)

In this August 1957 image, CTA Met car No. 2920 approaches the eastern end of the Kenwood "L" at Forty-second Place. This was one of the only locations along the line that used a steel structure. The yard at the end of the line was largely unused after 1949. Service was abandoned soon after this picture was taken. The photographer was standing on a nearby embankment, which joined with the "L" nearby.

A pair of 4000-series "L" cars are shown at the Kenwood Terminal at Forty-second Place and Oakenwald Avenue on November 12, 1928. The tower controlled train movements. The ground-level freight tracks at right belonged to the Chicago Junction Railway. There was a coal yard here, and coal is piled up underneath the "L."

A Kenwood shuttle car is pictured at the Forty-second Place terminal on June 12, 1957. The Chicago Junction Railway and the CTA could not come to terms regarding rent or station upkeep. This, plus declining ridership, led to the abandonment of the branch. (Lawrence H. Boehuring photograph.)

Ross Harano is pictured in 1945 as a toddler with his uncle Susumu Okamoto (1919–2005) in front of the Kenwood "L" terminal at Forty-second Place and Oakenwald Avenue. The extended Harano family lived across the street from the terminal from 1945 to 1961 after being confined to an internment camp during World War II. The internment of Japanese Americans was a dark chapter in US history. Seven of Ross Harano's uncles, including Susumu Okamoto, volunteered and served with distinction in the US military during the war. (Ross Harano.)

The interior of former Met "L" car No. 2872 is shown while it was operating on the Kenwood shuttle in 1953. After the CTA stopped using wooden "L" cars in 1957, No. 2872 was moved to Kimball Yard on the Ravenswood "L" branch and used as a stationary locker room until the 1980s. This car has been saved and is now at the Illinois Railway Museum in Union. Note the sideways seating, which has not proven to be very popular on newer CTA cars. (William C. Hoffman photograph.)

Here, CTA Met car No. 2907 is at Indiana Avenue running the Kenwood shuttle on the last day of service, November 30, 1957 (this was also the last day for regular passenger service for wooden "L" cars). Although it took over a decade for the CTA to replace the wooden "L" cars, New York did not retire theirs until October 4, 1969.

This is an inbound Normal Park shuttle car between Harvard station on the Englewood branch and Stewart Junction. Car No. 223 was made by Jewett in 1902 for the South Side "L." The Harvard Theater (lower right) was at 6312 South Harvard Avenue. The theater, which seated 720, opened in 1915 and closed in the 1960s; it has since been demolished. Next to it is one of the thousands of mom-and-pop groceries that used to dot Chicago's neighborhoods.

A 1949 Normal Park shuttle train is pictured on the inbound track at Sixty-third Street and Harvard Avenue, ready to proceed south. Since the Normal Park branch was so close to Harvard Avenue, trains did not have to cross over to the southbound track. This short branch was abandoned in 1954.

The Normal Park "L" ended at Sixty-ninth Street between Normal and Parnell Avenues. This was the farthest south the "L" went until the Dan Ryan line opened in 1969. The Dan Ryan line was not intended to replace the South Side "L" but did divert much of its ridership. Still, paired with the Lake Street "L" as the CTA Green Line, the South Side "L" remains an integral part of the CTA system. (Edward Frank Jr. photograph.)

Two

THE LAKE STREET "L"

Lake Street "L" Forney-type steam engine No. 5 is shown in the mid-1890s near the enginehouse at Crawford Avenue (now Pulaski Road). The two Chicago "L" operators who used steam power chose beefed-up versions of locomotives that had proven themselves on the New York elevated lines. The engines and coaches were light and had to start and stop quickly, sometimes in as short a distance as two city blocks. Loco No. 9, a sister locomotive to No. 5, is now at the Museum of Transportation in St. Louis. (Chicago Transit Authority Historical Collection.)

The Lake Street "L" is shown under construction at Rockwell Street (2600 W.) in 1892. (Chicago Transit Authority Historical Collection.)

This 1890s postcard shows the Lake Street "L" crossing the Chicago River at a time when steam provided the power. This view is looking north with Wolf Point in the distance. The swing bridge was replaced by a bascule type in 1916 and rehabilitated in 1995. (William Shapotkin Collection.)

The "L" station at Lake Street and Ashland Boulevard was built in the Queen Anne style in 1892–1893 and is one of the original stations on the line. Looking east, this is how the station appeared in 1972. Lyon and Healy, makers of harps and other instruments, is in the distance. One can also see the unfinished IBM Building designed by Ludwig Mies van der Rohe (1886–1969) next to Marina Towers.

Prior to the unification of the four "L" companies, Lake and Paulina Streets was the only place where two competing lines crossed each other. In 1913, the two lines were connected by a transfer station, since riders could now switch between lines for free. This is a view of the Lake Street Transfer station, which closed on February 25, 1951, when Humboldt Park became a shuttle and Logan Square trains began using the new Dearborn-Milwaukee subway.

Built in 1909 by Brill, CTA car No. 3164 is at the Hamlin station on the Lake Street "L" in August 1948 and is signed as an "A" train. This was a "local" station just two blocks east of Pulaski Road. It survived for a few years after the CTA instituted A/B skip-stop service on Lake Street in 1948 but was closed and demolished in 1956. The middle track was used for car storage and, before the CTA era, by express trains.

On December 6, 1952, a three-car train of CTA 1700-series cars descends the ramp between Laramie Avenue and Central Avenue on the Lake Street "L," bringing it down to street level. The "L" structure stopped at Laramie Avenue (5200 W.) and ran at ground level west of here. A permanent alignment along South Boulevard in Oak Park was established in 1901. (Robert Selle photograph.)

October 27, 1962, was the last day of ground-level operation on the CTA Lake Street "L." The following day, service was elevated via the adjacent Chicago & North Western (C&NW) embankment. Here, a pair of 4000s is heading west on South Boulevard at Kenilworth Avenue. The C&NW tracks were raised in 1909, but it took another 53 years for the Lake Street "L" to join them.

This is a c. 1930 view looking east at Lake Street and Ridgeland Avenue when the Lake Street "L" ran on the ground. The Chicago Rapid Transit Company put advertisements on the steps leading into ground-level stations.

The Wisconsin Avenue (later Marion Street) station in Oak Park served as the western end of the Lake Street "L" when this picture was taken in 1909. The express train at right is heading east since the line ran left-handed until 1913. At the far right, part of the Chicago & North Western's commuter station can be seen, shortly before that railroad was elevated onto a new embankment. (*Chicago Daily News* collection, DN-0055415, Chicago History Museum.)

At 8:05 a.m. on Thursday, March 31, 1955, Chicago & North Western steam locomotive No. 654 (4-6-2), with commuter train, headed east at high speed at Oak Park Avenue in suburban Oak Park. The embankment here was wide enough to make room for the Lake Street "L" seven years later. (Robert Selle photograph.)

In June 1963, several months after the CTA elevated the Lake Street "L" onto the Chicago & North Western embankment, a four-car train made up of "circus wagons," a nickname for CTA's experimental high-speed cars, made a rare appearance at Harlem Avenue (7200 W.), the end of the line. This view is looking east.

The Lake Street "L" (now the CTA Green Line) finally received a proper end-of-the-line yard in 1964 in suburban Forest Park. In this March 1993 photograph, various cars in the 2000-series are shown along with a Metra commuter train on the adjacent Union Pacific West Line (the former Chicago & North Western). The two lines run parallel for two and a half miles east of here. (Bruce C. Nelson photograph.)

On July 28, 2020, this CTA Green Line train was at Marion Street and South Boulevard, the current terminal. There is another station entrance on Harlem Avenue. In 1998, a new entrance was carved out of the embankment, connecting with Metra's Oak Park commuter station on the Union Pacific West Line.

Three

THE METROPOLITAN "L"

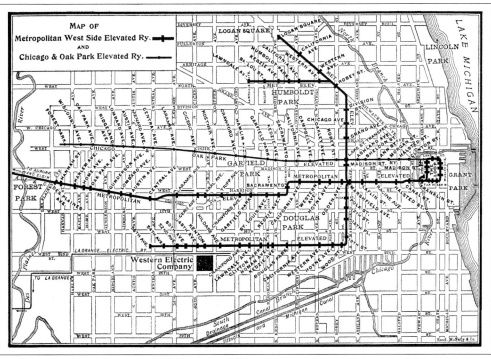

The Metropolitan West Side and Lake Street "L's were competitors, as their tracks were relatively close to each other. While Lake Street's early attempts at branch lines were a failure, the Met planned several right from the start, and they all went into service within a short period of time. This map is from 1913. Douglas Park did not reach its full extent until 1924. The Garfield Park "L" was later extended to Bellwood and Westchester using trackage owned by the Chicago, Aurora & Elgin interurban.

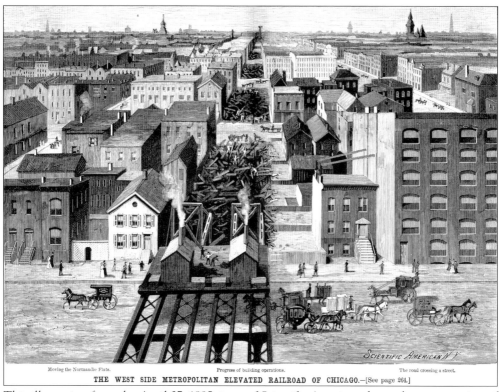

Moving the Normandie Flats.   Progress of building operations.   The road crossing a street.

THE WEST SIDE METROPOLITAN ELEVATED RAILROAD OF CHICAGO.—[See page 264.]

This illustration from the April 27, 1895, issue of *Scientific American* shows the construction of the Metropolitan West Side Elevated on private property down the centers of blocks, in contrast to previous "L"s that were either built above city streets or adjacent to alleyways.

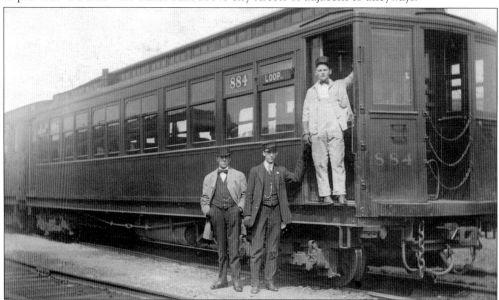

A train crew has just taken a six-car Met "L" train, headed by car No. 884, out of the yard prior to a run around 1910. Car No. 884 was built by Pullman in 1906. When the four "L" companies combined their operations in 1913, this car became No. 1884.

A Met "L" conductor is pictured here in the early 1900s. Although the city became more diverse, "L" hiring practices did not. African Americans were not hired as motormen or conductors until 1943, and then only due to federal pressure. Women were not hired for these positions until 1974. Much progress has been made toward inclusion.

The elevated structure, shown on February 11, 1952, in this image looking east, connected the Met main line with the Loop "L." The track at left, going straight, led to the Wells Street Terminal. A new station, for Met use only, was built at Franklin and Van Buren Streets. Lower Wacker Drive construction meant tearing down this part of the "L," and a new connection to the Loop was built through Wells Street Terminal.

A two-car Met "L" train is shown crossing the Chicago River just west of the Loop in July 1951. This bridge was actually two bridges side by side, as there were four tracks. In case something happened to one bridge, the other could still be used.

The four-track Met main line is shown in this picture looking west toward the Canal Street station in 1924. Here, the "L" went over Union Station's train shed. The shape of the 547 West Jackson Boulevard Building, at right, was partly determined by the curving "L." This was also the Chicago, Burlington & Quincy Railroad's headquarters from 1911 to 1970. The middle train is signed as a "Shopper's Special"—nomenclature that the CTA was still using in the late 1950s. (Chicago Transit Authority Historical Collection.)

Two Garfield Park trains pass on a curvy section of "L" west of the Canal Street station on April 13, 1957. The nearby manufacturing district included the Trav-Ler Radio Corporation, founded in 1921, which made table radios, record players, and television sets.

In this September 5, 1953, view looking west from the CTA Racine Avenue station on the old Metropolitan main line, the massive Throop Street Shops are at right. A Chicago, Aurora & Elgin train approaches, heading toward the Loop. Soon, this all had to go to make way for the Congress (now Eisenhower) Expressway. (Robert Selle photograph.)

This view is looking west at Marshfield Junction, where all Met lines came together. A wooden Chicago, Aurora & Elgin train at the auxiliary platform is made up of cars purchased secondhand from the North Shore Line in 1946. The train is heading eastbound. The tracks to the right went to Logan Square and Humboldt Park, while the tracks to the left went to Douglas Park. When these tracks were removed in 1953 to make room for the Congress Expressway, the north and south tracks were bridged to form what was later called the Paulina Connector. An inbound Logan Square "L" train is visible at right.

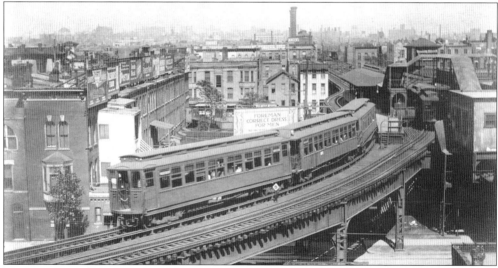

A Met "L" train heads northwest from Marshfield Junction toward Logan Square and Humboldt Park around 1910. This view is looking east. One of the signs advertises Postum, a popular coffee substitute invented in 1895.

This is the Oak Park Avenue terminal at the outer end of the Douglas Park "L," looking west, around 1949. The apartment building at right is still standing. The line was cut back to Fifty-fourth Avenue in 1952. Expresses alternated with locals. Douglas began using A/B skip-stop service on December 9, 1951. Note the Burma Shave sign at right.

The Douglas Park Fiftieth Avenue station opened in 1910, when the line was extended to Central Avenue (5600 W.). After it closed in 1978, the entire station house and platform were disassembled and moved to the Illinois Railway Museum, where its interior is shown in this photograph taken on September 14, 2019.

William C. Hoffman took this picture of the Garfield Park "L" at Western Avenue, looking northwest, on October 19, 1953. Remarkably, trains ran here until as late as September 27. Two and a half miles of "L" that were directly in the path of the Congress Expressway were demolished in 1953–1954.

In this mid-1950s image, a two-car train of flat-door CTA 6000s heads west on Garfield Park temporary trackage at Paulina Street (1700 W.), about to cross under tracks now used by the CTA's Pink Line. The temporary right-of-way was used from 1953 to 1958.

Several CTA Garfield Park "L" stations were closed during highway construction between 1953 and 1958. On September 26, 1953, this four-car train of wooden Met cars made a Loop-bound stop at California Avenue. Westbound service here had already been shifted to nearby temporary tracks on Van Buren Street on September 20. Eastbound trains were moved there on September 27, and the station was torn down, for it was in the way of the Congress Expressway footprint. (Robert Selle photograph.)

The Pulaski Road station on the Garfield Park "L" was typical of Met "L" architecture, of which very few examples remain. Pulaski was not affected by highway construction and remained in use until the new Congress median line opened in 1958. It was also an important transfer point between the "L" and streetcars. CTA streetcar No. 1710, operating on the Madison–Fifth branch line, is turning north onto Pulaski Road from Fifth Avenue on July 5, 1953, using gauntlet trackage separate from that used by northbound Pulaski Road streetcars. (Robert Selle photograph.)

The old Cicero Avenue station on the Garfield Park "L" is shown in this photograph looking east around July 1, 1957. To the west, Laramie was at ground level, and to the east, Kilbourn station was higher, as the "L" crossed other railroads.

The Garfield Park structure ended at Cicero Avenue (4800 W.), and a ramp took the "L" down to grade level toward Laramie Avenue (5200 W.). This must be an early picture, since the area around the "L" is largely unbuilt. Laramie Yard was behind the photographer. This section of "L" was torn down shortly after the CTA opened the Congress line in 1958.

Both CTA and Chicago, Aurora & Elgin (CA&E) trains are visible in this July 8, 1953, photograph taken at Laramie Avenue (5200 W.), looking east along the Garfield Park "L." A little over two months later, the CA&E interurban cut back service to Forest Park a few miles west of here.

This view from the opposite end of Laramie Yard is looking west from Lavergne Avenue (5000 W.) around 1910. The Laramie Avenue station, tower, and shops are in the distance, about two blocks away. Met car No. 761 was built by Barney & Smith in 1898 and rebuilt as a work car in 1902. It was later renumbered to S-201.

This picture, taken on November 24, 1957, shows Laramie Tower and the Shops building. By this time, there were many old wood cars in storage, including No. 1763 and No. 1806, Northwestern "L" cars recently retired from service on the Evanston branch. There are several automobiles present, including a Ford and a Buick exiting the Congress Expressway, which ended here between 1955 and 1960. (Robert Selle photograph.)

A six-car train of Met cars heads west on the Garfield Park "L" between Central Avenue (5600 W.) and Austin Boulevard (6000 W.), where the line ran just south of Columbus Park. Freight tracks of the Baltimore & Ohio Chicago Terminal were at right. This is now the location of the Eisenhower Expressway, which opened here in October 1960.

On September 6, 1935, this photographer looked along Oak Park Avenue at Harrison Street in suburban Oak Park. A Chicago & West Towns bus is headed north on Oak Park Avenue, having just crossed the tracks of two railroads—the Baltimore & Ohio Chicago Terminal (a freight line) and the Chicago, Aurora & Elgin interurban. CRT Garfield Park and Westchester trains also ran here. The Congress (now Eisenhower) Expressway opened here in 1960. (William Shapotkin Collection.)

This unusual photograph was taken on April 14, 1957, from the wooden trestle used by Garfield Park "L" trains to loop around at Forest Park from 1953 to 1959. CTA and Chicago, Aurora & Elgin tracks were separated and looped around each other. The view looks to the north. In the background are the Chicago Great Western freight tracks, abandoned in the early 1970s. The terminal has been rebuilt twice since then. A two-car train of CTA "Baldy" 4000s (built around 1914) negotiates the loop. The Altenheim retirement home (left), built in 1886, is at 7824 West Madison Street.

A three-car wooden "L" train, headed by No. 2918, crosses DesPlaines Avenue in Forest Park, heading westbound into what was then a new terminal on October 10, 1953. During the rebuilding of this line for expressway construction, these tracks were moved slightly to the south, and the diner at right was torn down. (Robert Selle photograph.)

On April 4, 1959, a westbound CTA Congress–Milwaukee "A" train crosses DesPlaines Avenue in Forest Park over temporary trackage. Interstate 290 is under construction here, and this portion of the highway opened in 1960. The tracks shown here were south of where the line crosses DesPlaines Avenue today. The CTA temporary tracks are about where the westbound lanes of Interstate 290 are now.

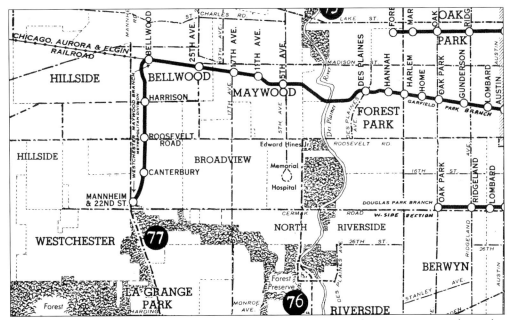

By the mid-1920s, the Samuel Insull empire owned all three major Chicago area interurbans plus the "L." The North Shore Line was modernized with a bypass route to the west of its original line. Insull planned to do the same thing for the Chicago, Aurora & Elgin, and the Westchester "L" was part of a plan to extend service to present-day Oakbrook. Mannheim Road and Twenty-second Street was as far as this plan ever got, as it was stymied by the Great Depression. To reach the Westchester branch, "L" trains had to run on the Chicago, Aurora & Elgin main line to Bellwood.

The Westchester branch diverged from the Chicago, Aurora & Elgin main line (shown here running parallel to the Chicago Great Western) in Bellwood. This view is looking east. Since a 4000 is paired with a wood car, this picture may date to before 1943, when all of CRT's steel cars were needed for the new State Street Subway.

The new Westchester "L" station at Bellwood, just south of the Chicago, Aurora & Elgin main line, is pictured here on February 8, 1926. Regular service did not begin until October 1 of that year.

A southbound Westchester train is shown crossing Madison Street in Bellwood, where Marshall Avenue begins today. The house at right is still standing. The Bellwood station was just north of here. This picture was taken just west of Bellwood Avenue.

In this April 28, 1929, view looking north, a steam shovel digs an underpass for Westchester trains at the Roosevelt Road station. The line was extended to Mannheim Road and Twenty-second Street (now Cermak Road) on December 1, 1930. Development started here in the late 1920s but was delayed by the Great Depression and did not resume until after World War II. The CTA discontinued "L" service here on December 9, 1951. Ridership was low; rent was being paid to the Chicago, Aurora & Elgin; and it was decided that buses could provide adequate service.

This June 21, 1958, view is looking northeast at the new "L" ramp to connect Douglas Park trains to the Congress line and the Dearborn-Milwaukee subway. Even though the track connection was yet unfinished, the change began the following day. From 1954 to 1958, Douglas trains continued north from here to a connection with the Lake Street "L." Now, the CTA Pink Line, Douglas's replacement, also uses the Lake Street routing. (Robert Selle photograph.)

Old and new west side "L's coexisted for just one day—June 21, 1958. At right, the CTA offered free rides to Cicero Avenue (4800 W.) on its new rapid transit line, running in the median of the Congress Expressway. This was also the final day of service on the Garfield Park "L" at left. This view is looking northeast at the Halsted Street station, which had four tracks prior to expressway construction. Two were removed in 1954. Perhaps not coincidentally, this was also the last day for streetcar service in Chicago. (Robert Selle photograph.)

Car No. 2100, at the rear of this outbound Logan Square train leaving Damen, was built by Pullman in 1894 as car No. 100. The train is leaving the Damen station headed northwest around 1949. The distant tower controlled movements with the Humboldt Park branch.

The Met's Logan Square "L" terminal is shown here in 1908. The Centennial Monument, Logan Square's most distinctive feature, was not built until 1918, commemorating the 100th anniversary of Illinois's statehood. Logan Square Auditorium was built to the north of the "L" in 1915.

The Logan Square "L" terminal is pictured here on May 10, 1958. Twelve years later, this station was replaced by a subway as part of an extension to Jefferson Park. Now, trains go all the way to O'Hare Airport, several miles farther. (Laurence H. Boehuring photograph.)

The Met conductor at right in this c. 1910 image is Ray Robert Kretschmer (1889–1960), shown at the Logan Square terminal. He later worked for the post office. This photograph was provided by Kretschmer's grandson Bruce Henry.

The Humboldt Park "L" was a branch of the Metropolitan running east-west for about two miles, just north of North Avenue (1600 N.) to Lawndale Avenue (3700 W.). Service began in 1895, but plans to extend the line farther west were never realized. The CTA abandoned it in 1952, figuring people could take the North Avenue trolley bus instead. Here, three nattily dressed Humboldt Park conductors are pictured around 1910.

CRT car No. 4102 and its "plus one" are heading west, having just crossed the Chicago River on the four-track Met main line. They would serve both Logan Square and Humboldt Park, as this two-car train would split at Damen and North Avenues. Canal Street station had walkways directly connecting to Union Station. It closed in June 1958, when the Congress median line opened. No. 4102, the head car, was built in 1914 and retired in 1964. The center doors on these cars were closed off and never used.

This is the Met "L" station at Madison Street and Paulina Street, looking north. The presence of new 6000s here dates the picture to between August 1950 and February 1951, shortly before the Dearborn-Milwaukee subway went into service. The Lake Street transfer station is visible in the distance.

The Madison and Paulina "L" station is shown on November 26, 1928, in this view looking west. The structure was later rebuilt for the CTA Pink Line, although there is no station here now. Chicago Stadium opened to the west of here on March 28, 1929. It has since been replaced by the United Center.

This view is looking east from Madison and Paulina Streets in 1937. The large building in the background is in the triangle of Ogden-Ashland-Madison, and starting in 1956, it had a 34-foot-tall, illuminated Turtle Wax turtle on top of it. The Lindy Theater at 1710 West Madison Street opened in 1909 as the Palais Royal. It was renamed in 1928 after Charles Lindbergh became an international celebrity following his nonstop flight from New York to Paris in 1927. *Hell's Angels* was a 1930 film rereleased after Jean Harlow died, playing with a Gene Autry Western and the Republic serial *Dick Tracy*. A new Chicago Surface Lines PCC streetcar is heading east. Fast service on the Madison line made it competitive with the west side "L's."

A view of the Humboldt Park "L" is looking west from Western Avenue on January 26, 1931. This branch closed in 1952, although portions of the structure remained into the early 1960s for possible midday use by the Chicago, Aurora & Elgin for train storage.

Lawndale Avenue (3700 W.) was as far west as the Humboldt Park "L" ever went. If extended, it could have become one of CTA's most popular lines. There was no money for this in the 1950s, so the CTA decided to close it. The neighborhood lobbied to save the line but only succeeded in delaying its abandonment for a year. There was no yard here, so cars were stored on tracks near the single platform terminal. The "M" on the tower likely stands for "MET." This picture dates to around 1949.

The CTA wanted to close the Humboldt Park branch when the Dearborn-Milwaukee subway opened in 1951. Instead, it became a shuttle operation for about a year. This small platform was part of a very inconvenient and convoluted connection with the Damen Avenue station, and riders had to walk through narrow walkways, over some distance, and walk up and down a few times to change trains. The line was abandoned on May 4, 1952.

Accidents will happen and sometimes did over the years, as seen in this c. 1910 view. Here, two Met "L" trains collided while one was crossing over to the other track. The view is looking west from Kedzie Avenue (3200 W.) on the Humboldt Park branch.

On June 21, 1958, Robert Selle took this picture from the front window of a Douglas Park train heading northbound near the connection with the Lake Street "L." The following day, Douglas connected with the Congress–Milwaukee line. The tracks at left were the old "L" route leading to Logan Square and Humboldt Park, which had been out of service since 1951 and were torn down in 1964. Now, CTA Pink Line trains use the same connection at right.

One bit of the old Paulina "L" remains and is used as a signal bridge for Metra commuter trains. This is how it looked on June 7, 2020.

Over the decades, major parts of the Met "L" were rebuilt, replaced, or abandoned for a variety of reasons, to the point where few original sections remain today. This is one of those sections, running parallel to Milwaukee Avenue at the Damen Avenue station in the Wicker Park neighborhood on August 21, 1970. A six-car train of CTA "L" cars, in the 6600-series, heads northwest. The building directly behind the train, at 1551 North Damen Avenue, was home to the well-known Double Door rock club from 1994 to 2017. The Rolling Stones played there in 1997.

Four

THE NORTHWESTERN "L"

The Northwestern Elevated Railroad opened in 1900, going as far north as Wilson Avenue (4600 N.). The Ravenswood branch followed in 1907, with the outer mile built at grade level. No franchise was required, as that segment was entirely built on private land—there were not yet streets to cross. Rapid development followed the "L." In 1908, the Northwestern made a deal with the Milwaukee Road to take over the latter's commuter rail line on a lease basis. This was known as the "Evanston Extension," gradually elevated in Chicago and Evanston. Service was extended to Linden Avenue in Wilmette in 1912. Eventually, the main line had four tracks nearly all the way between Chicago Avenue (800 N.) and Howard Street (7600 N.), with express and local service. Above is an early view of the Northwestern "L" just north of the Loop. Kinzie Street station opened in 1900 and served the old Chicago & North Western terminal here. After that was relocated in 1911, ridership dropped off, and the "L" station was replaced by a new one at Grand Avenue in 1921. After the Merchandise Mart was built on the site of the old terminal, a new "L" station opened here in 1930.

The Merchandise Mart, one of the largest buildings in the world, opened on May 5, 1930. Its "L" station, shown under construction on October 22, 1930, opened on December 5, 1930. This image shows a view looking north.

The original station entrance at Chicago Avenue (800 N.), designed in an Italianate style by Walter Gibb, was used from 1900 to 2007. Here is how it looked on July 27, 2020.

CTA cars No. 4271 and No. 4272 headed up a northbound Evanston Express train passing through the Chicago Avenue station on June 26, 1958. These two cars, originally independent but converted to semipermanent "married pairs" in the 1950s, are still on CTA property and will soon celebrate their centennial. When the last of the 4000-series "L" cars were retired in 1973, they were chosen for preservation and are occasionally used for special events. (Robert Selle photograph.)

A northbound express is shown passing the Willow Street station (1800 N.) on the north-side main line. This small station, opened in 1905, was one of the only ones the Chicago Rapid Transit Company ever shuttered. It was located near where the State Street Subway incline to the "L" was built, which necessitated the closing of Willow Street on May 17, 1942, and its subsequent demolition.

Baseball season was in full swing on September 2, 1968, when this southbound CTA Jackson Park–Howard "L" train stopped at Belmont Avenue. A sign on the train told riders there was a Cubs game that day. The Cubs played a doubleheader with the San Francisco Giants, who won the first game 8-4 behind the pitching of future Hall of Famer Juan Marichal. The second game was called at 6:41 p.m. on account of darkness and ended in a 1-1 tie (Wrigley Field did not have lights for night games until 1988). The two games were attended by 35,061 fans. After more than a century of use, the Belmont station was completely rebuilt in 2007. A flyover is now under construction that will keep Red, Brown, and Purple Line trains apart. (William Shapotkin Collection.)

The Northwestern Elevated Railroad

Ironically, the only station ever closed on the Ravenswood branch was its namesake—Ravenswood Avenue (4600 N., 1800 W.), a neighborhood station located in the middle of the block and set back from the street. When the branch opened in 1907, it was adjacent to the Chicago & North Western commuter line's Ravenswood station, which was later moved two blocks north. The CTA closed this station on August 1, 1949. (J.J. Sedelmaier Collection.)

In this August 1949 photograph, an outbound Ravenswood "A" train at Rockwell Street (2600 W.) has just descended a ramp from the Western Avenue station. Line extensions were built quickly and cheaply at ground level, with the expectation that they would be elevated later if ridership increased. Despite having good ridership, the outer one mile of the Ravenswood route (today's Brown Line) still runs at grade.

This is the original Craftsman-style Ravenswood terminal at Lawrence Avenue (4800 N.) and Kimball Avenue (3400 W.) when it was new. The station building closely resembled the Lower Wilson entrance on the Northwestern main line. Both were designed by architect Arthur U. Gerber and built in 1907.

This is an uncropped version of the picture on the book's cover. Two sets of conductors and motormen check their watches and share a moment before their scheduled departures at Lawrence and Kimball in 1950. This image shows the other side of the original Craftsman-style station entrance shown in the previous photograph. The Kimball station was remodeled in 1974 and 2007.

Montrose Tower (4400 N.), at right, controlled movements at Wilson Avenue. Looking south, one can see the four-track Northwestern "L," which accommodated expresses and locals. The ramp at right connected to Buena Yard, where electric locomotives of the "L" interchanged freight with the Milwaukee Road until 1973.

On March 5, 1907, the new lower level "L" station at Wilson Avenue and Evanston Avenue (later Broadway) opened with its modest headhouse designed by Arthur U. Gerber. It was originally used for express trains, while locals boarded on the "L" structure above. All service terminated here until the following year when the "L" was extended at ground level to Evanston. The lower level station closed in 1949. (*Chicago Daily News* collection, DN-0004736, Chicago History Museum.)

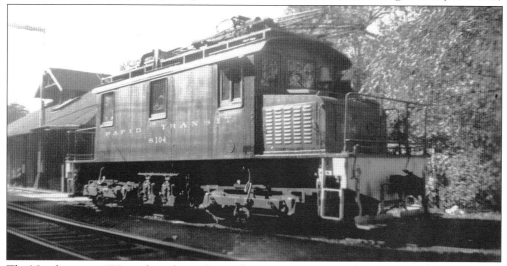

The Northwestern "L" purchased two electric locomotives in 1920 when it assumed responsibility for freight operations north of Montrose Avenue (4400 N.) from the Milwaukee Road. Locomotive S-104 was built by Baldwin-Westinghouse in August 1920, and the two locomotives handled the hauling up to the end of freight service on April 30, 1973. In the rear is Milwaukee Road's former Graceland station, which closed in 1917 (when commuter rail service ended on this branch).

This image looking north shows Wilson Yard and Shops in August 1963. The yard opened in 1900 along with the Northwestern "L." After Howard Yard opened in 1919, Wilson diminished in importance as more and more trains terminated north of here. Howard gradually expanded, while Wilson was aging. Wilson's main functions were transferred to Howard in 1993. Wilson Yard and Shops were destroyed by fire on October 26, 1996, and not replaced. (Craig Berndt Collection.)

Several wooden "L" cars, some with broken windows, are seen in dead storage at the Wilson Avenue Lower Yard in August 1956, awaiting scrapping. Wilson's need for a lower yard diminished over the years. Trains were no longer boarded there after 1949, and the lower yard tracks were phased out in the late 1950s. The view is looking north, and the back of the McJunkin Building (constructed in 1923) can be seen at right. The yard tracks ended at Wilson Avenue (4600 N.).

This picture is looking west along Wilson Avenue from Broadway on January 21, 1929. The track in the background was used for freight. Wilson was an important transfer point with the North Shore Line interurban, and "L" service here helped spur the rapid development of the Uptown neighborhood in the 1920s. It became a mecca for entertainment with the Green Mill, Uptown Theatre, Riviera Theatre, and Aragon Ballroom.

A ceremony was held at the Wilson Avenue "L" station in December 1922 to mark the start of work on what became the new Uptown Union Station the following year. This meant the demolition of the short-lived, triangular-shaped Stohr Arcade building, designed in 1909 by noted architect Frank Lloyd Wright. Workers with pickaxes are tearing it apart. Wright did not count it among his most notable works. (*Chicago Daily News* collection, DN-0075220, Chicago History Museum.)

The Uptown Union Station, designed by Arthur U. Gerber, became the new "L" entrance in 1923. The station entrance at Wilson Avenue and Broadway was recently restored to its original appearance in conjunction with the complete rebuilding of the station, tracks, and structure; the new station opened on September 20, 2017. This picture is from June 6, 2020.

Service at the Birchwood "L" station in the Rogers Park neighborhood was hastily moved to this temporary station between Chase Avenue and Sherwin Avenue at midnight on July 1, 1915, as part of the project to elevate the tracks onto a new embankment. The view is looking north and shows a section of embankment under construction up ahead. Once the "L" was raised, this station was relocated to Jarvis Avenue (7400 N.). (*Chicago Daily News* collection, DN-0064743, Chicago History Museum.)

A new "L" station at Lawrence Avenue (4800 N.) opened on February 27, 1923. The man holding the handrail is Britton I. Budd (1871–1965), who had a distinguished career starting with the Columbian Intramural Railway in 1893. He rose through the ranks and became president of the Metropolitan "L" in 1910. Budd eventually served as president of the "L" and the North Shore Line. (Chicago Transit Authority Historical Collection.)

Here is a World War II–era view of the southbound freight track at Lawrence Avenue, which connected to the Buena Yard. "L" trains also used this track, but south of the station, four tracks were reduced to two going into Wilson Avenue. The small building just past the platform is Lawrence Tower, which controlled the interlocking switches. Note the penny scale at the station.

In this image looking north from the Howard "L" station around 1930, the North Shore Line's new Skokie Valley Route, also used by Niles Center "L" trains, is at left. The tracks in the middle went to the Evanston "L," also used by the North Shore Line's Shore Line Route. Howard Yard is at right.

When the CTA revised service on August 1, 1949, Howard became the most important north-side terminal. Work to add a turning loop to the yard began in July 1949 and was finished on February 10, 1950.

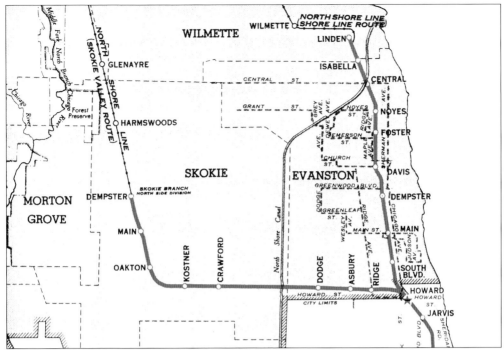

This is a 1941 Chicago Rapid Transit Company map of the Evanston and Skokie "L" branches. CTA service continues on both today, although the North Shore Line interurban quit in 1963.

The old Central Street Evanston terminal is shown here sometime between 1908 and 1912. Note the large number of trailers. At the station is a Chicago & Milwaukee Electric wood interurban—the predecessor of the North Shore Line. "L" service was extended to Linden Avenue in Wilmette in 1912 and a new yard added. The "L" was elevated here starting in 1928, and the current station opened in 1931.

Work was underway on elevating the north portion of Evanston's "L" at Noyes Street (looking south) in this picture taken on August 10, 1928. Between October and December of that year, northbound traffic was rerouted onto the new embankment. Once the work was completed, southbound traffic shifted there too, at which time the ground-level tracks and stations were removed. Note how there are two sets of tracks at right so freight trains could clear the station platform.

The Calvary "L" station in Evanston, which was adjacent to a cemetery, opened in 1908 at ground level but was elevated by 1910. It had low ridership and was one of only two flag stops on the "L," and anyone on the platform had to signal an approaching train by yanking a cord attached to a semaphore. It closed in 1931 and was replaced by a stop at South Boulevard a few blocks to the north. This is one of the few pictures of Calvary in existence.

On September 9, 1928, what was reportedly the first "L" train on newly raised tracks headed northbound at Central Street in Evanston. This view is looking east. The southbound track is still at grade level.

The Central Street "L" station is shown under construction in 1930. The terra-cotta facade created by Arthur U. Gerber combines Doric and Beaux-Arts styles.

The Central Street facade is pictured here on June 6, 2020.

The Isabella station was just a few blocks away from the northern end of the Evanston "L" at Linden Avenue in Wilmette. Service was extended here on April 1, 1912. This image shows the station (and the still undeveloped area around it) on June 27, 1928, and the view is looking northeast. For a time starting in 1930, inbound riders had to signal approaching trains to get them to stop. The CTA closed Isabella on July 16, 1973, and all traces of the station were removed soon after. It is fondly remembered as the location where Bob Newhart got off the "L" in the opening credits of *The Bob Newhart Show*. (J.J. Sedelmaier Collection.)

The North Shore Line interurban tracks connected to the CTA at Linden Avenue in Wilmette, just east of the terminal at the north end of the Evanston branch. In this July 25, 1955, photograph, the track connection with the CTA has just been severed, as service on the North Shore Line's Shore Line Route was abandoned the previous day. (Joseph Canfield photograph; David Stanley Collection.)

Samuel Insull's North Shore Line built the Skokie Valley Route in the 1920s to speed up the interurban compared to its existing Shore Line Route. Rapid transit service was extended to Dempster Street in Niles Center (now Skokie) on March 28, 1925. (Chicago Transit Authority Historical Collection.)

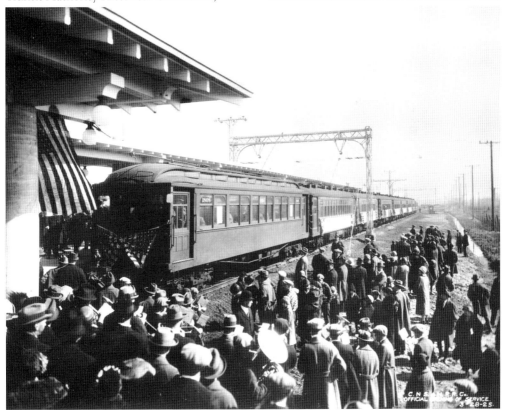

A single-car Niles Center train is shown in the open cut in Evanston.

The new Dodge Avenue station on the Niles Center branch—pictured on March 28, 1925—was designed in a Beaux-Arts style by Arthur U. Gerber. After the branch closed in 1948, it was rented out to an electrical supply firm. It was removed in the 1980s after it fell into disrepair. (J.J. Sedelmaier Collection.)

The Gerber-designed Asbury Avenue station on the Niles Center "L" had a Mediterranean influence in keeping with some North Shore Line stations that earned the nickname "Insull Spanish." It is shown on February 27, 1925, shortly before the line opened. The station entrance, on a bridge, had a more conventional entrance somewhat like the Dodge Avenue station. After 1948, a small grocery store used the building, which was removed in the 1980s. (J.J. Sedelmaier Collection.)

Asbury's attractive interior is pictured on April 13, 1925. (J.J. Sedelmaier Collection.)

At Dempster Street, the "L" had pocket tracks south of the station entrance. Car No. 1045 is in the pocket, and the North Shore tracks are in the foreground.

CRT car No. 1804, shown here at Crawford Avenue and East Prairie Road, has just changed over from overhead wire to third rail on its inbound journey. This car was originally a trailer. The station had entrances from both streets, so the station house was between them. Its design was a combination of Prairie style and vernacular bungalow. The station remained after the 1948 "L" abandonment but was removed once the Skokie Swift started in 1964, as it created a blind spot for motormen on the high-speed cars.

A CTA single-car unit equipped with an airfoil pan trolley is shown navigating the Oakton Curve on the Skokie Swift on December 11, 1976. The Swift (now the Yellow Line) duplicated the Niles Center route but with no intermediate stops and added a large park-and-ride lot at Dempster. (William Shapotkin Collection.)

The North Shore Line's Dempster Street station, shown here on June 6, 2020, is considered Arthur U. Gerber's greatest work. After it opened in 1925, it remained in use until its 1963 abandonment. The old station was converted to retail use, and the CTA built a small new station nearby when the Skokie Swift began in 1964. Fortunately, the station was preserved and moved 130 feet east to allow for a bus turnaround.

The Oakton Street station closely resembled Dempster and was in use from 1925 to 1948. It was demolished shortly after the Skokie Swift began running in 1964. (J.J. Sedelmaier Collection.)

A new CTA station opened at Oakton Street on April 30, 2012, making it the only stop on the CTA Yellow Line between Dempster and Howard. On July 27, 2020, CTA cars No. 5523–No. 5524 depart the station headed southbound.

Five

THE UNION LOOP

This is a c. 1951 CTA track map of the Loop. The State Street Subway is also shown but the Dearborn-Milwaukee Subway is not. Some Loop stations had continuous platforms—a strategy employed to address overcrowding and congestion by allowing for longer trains with more places to berth them. Towers and stations were numbered, starting with Tower 8 at Van Buren and Wells Streets. In 1955, it was replaced by Tower 22 a bit to the north.

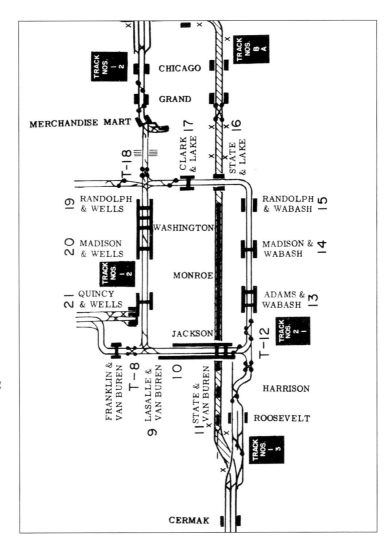

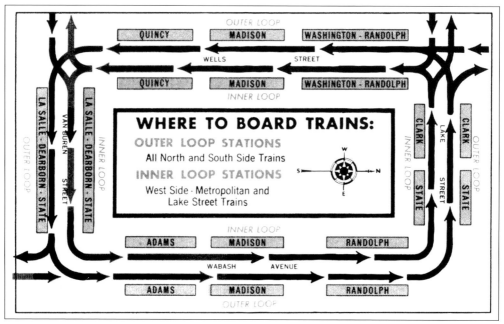

From 1913 to 1969, trains on the Loop ran in one direction: counterclockwise. Previously, Lake Street and Northwestern "L's" used left-hand running and later switched to right-hand instead. Starting in 1913, some north–south trains were through-routed, meaning they only used half of the Loop, thereby increasing capacity.

A view of the Loop "L" is shown here, looking west in 1905 along Van Buren Street at Wabash Avenue. Trains were then running bidirectionally, with left-hand running. Thus, the Lake Street train closest to Tower 12, on the outer track, is heading away from the photographer, closely following a Northwestern "L," while a Metropolitan train on the inner track heads toward the photographer.

The Wabash leg of the Loop is pictured prior to the 1913 service change that made it unidirectional. A Northwestern "L" car is turning east onto Van Buren Street next to Tower 12 and running left-handed. For many decades, Wabash Avenue was Chicago's "music row." The station in the distance is Adams and Wabash.

Car No. 1109 heads up a northbound Evanston Express train at Jackson Boulevard and Wabash Avenue in this 1940s image. Skokie is mentioned on the sign, and Niles Center changed its name to Skokie in 1941. Kimball Pianos is at right. The station in the distance is at Congress Street and Wabash Avenue and closed in the CTA's major service revision on August 1, 1949. It was removed in the early 1950s as Congress was widened for the expressway project. Then as now, it is never advisable to put one's head or arms outside the car window.

The Met did not use overhead wire, but there were some Met cars with trolley poles added for the 1926 Eucharistic Congress. This Douglas car is headed north at Randolph Street and Wabash Avenue, signed to go only to Lawndale. The temporary Ravenswood sign at left suggests this picture was taken in August 1949, just after the CTA's realignment of north–south service. The Randolph and Madison stations have been replaced by one at Washington Boulevard, located between them. This was also done on the Wells leg of the Loop. Now, the Loop has 8 stations instead of the 11 it once had.

Wooden car No. 3161 is shown leading a two-car Lake Street "B" train at Randolph Street and Wabash Avenue. This car was built by Brill in 1909 for the Lake Street "L" when it ran left-handed. That changed when the Loop became unidirectional in 1913. Note how the motorman's position is opposite that of most "L" cars.

A Lake "L" train of 2000-series cars, which were just two years old, is about to turn the corner from Wabash Avenue onto Lake Street in this 1966 image. This is the tightest radius curve on the system. On February 4, 1977, four "L" cars derailed here after colliding with another train. Two cars fell to the street below, killing 11 people and injuring 180. After this, steel was added to the outside of the structure to prevent a reoccurrence. In the distance at right, the *Chicago Sun-Times/Daily News* building is visible at 401 North Wabash Avenue. Built in the mid-1950s, it was demolished in 2004 and replaced with the Trump International Hotel and Tower.

Wooden car No. 305 is shown at the rear of a Wilson Avenue Local heading west at Clark and Lake station, through-routed from the south side. The Shreve Building, at right, stood at the northwest corner of Clark and Lake Streets and was built in 1875 in the wake of the Great Chicago Fire. Car No. 305 was built by Jewett in 1905.

A westbound Ravenswood "A" train is pictured at the old Clark and Lake station. The signs at right promote a stage version of *Mister Roberts* at the Erlanger Theatre, which starred John Forsyth, Jackie Cooper, and Cliff Robertson. Ravenswood A/B skip-stop service began on August 1, 1949, around the time this picture was taken. Transfer bridges were installed at Loop stations in 1913, when free transfers began between "L" lines.

The intersection at Lake Street and Wells Street was once the busiest in the world. In its busiest hour in 1927, a total of 224 trains with 1,244 cars passed by Tower 18. In this photograph taken on June 22, 1953, an Evanston train approaches at left while a North Shore train heads north and a Garfield Park "A" train turns the corner on the inner track. (Robert Selle photograph.)

As Loop ridership increased, platforms were extended to create more room to berth trains. Between 1924 and 1930, some stations on the Van Buren and Wells legs of the Loop were connected by continuous platforms, which may have inspired the long platforms in Chicago's first two subways. In this image looking north, Randolph and Wells is being extended to connect with Madison and Wells.

On June 14, 1955, wooden Met car No. 2912 and steel car No. 4224, both sporting fresh paint, were coupled for a charter trip on the south-side lines. They are shown at the Quincy Street and Wells Street station. (Robert Selle photograph.)

This is Wells and Van Buren Streets in the 1940s, showing the original connection between the Met lines and the Loop near Tower 8, looking north. Wells Street Terminal is at left; a walkway connected it to the Quincy and Wells Street station. The Insurance Exchange building is at right. (Joe L. Diaz photograph.)

A two-car Douglas Park train, heading toward Franklin and Van Buren Streets, is shown passing Tower 8 at Wells and Van Buren Streets in September 1949. One of the cars is gate car No. 2775, built by Barney and Smith in 1900. Cal's Liquors, a "shot and a beer" Charles Bukowski–type joint at 400 South Wells, closed in 2012 and was one of the last remnants of the "old" Loop.

This picture was taken in the same location as the last photograph but between 1955 and 1962. The "L" structure west of here and Tower 8 have been removed. The Garfield Park "L" connection to the Loop was relocated just north of here via the old Wells Street Terminal. The sign on this Lake Street train says the last stop is Clinton Street. The Insurance Exchange Building (at right) was erected in 1912.

Mayor Ed Kelly cuts the ribbon at the official opening of the State Street Subway on October 16, 1943. Forty years in the making, the subway helped save the Loop "L" by reducing congestion there. The City of Chicago built the subway, and the privately owned Chicago Rapid Transit Company agreed to use it.

The first official train in the State Street Subway is pictured on October 16, 1943. US Secretary of the Interior Harold Ickes (1874–1952), shown talking to CRT officials, was instrumental in getting the FDR administration to pay 45 percent of the subway's cost—among the earliest federal aid given to public transit. This predated the creation of the Chicago Transit Authority in 1945 and was an important step toward municipal ownership and transit unification.

A southbound CTA Douglas–Milwaukee "B" train is shown entering the Washington station on the Dearborn Subway in 1966. With the 1958 opening of the Congress median line, all the former Met "L" lines were through-routed via the Dearborn Subway, further diverting traffic from the Loop "L."

A Ravenswood "L" train is pictured at State and Lake Streets in April 1964. Fritzel's restaurant is at left. Ravenswood trains switched to the inner track after stopping on the outer track at Randolph and Wells Streets (except during weekday rush hours) from the 1950s until 1969, when the direction of the inner loop track was reversed.

In July 1969, Tower 18 at Lake and Wells Streets was demolished to permit a new track connection to be put in on the Loop "L." This was necessary so the CTA Lake Street "L" could be through-routed with the new Dan Ryan line that opened on September 28 of that year. A new tower is at left and has also since been replaced. From 1913 to 1969, trains ran counterclockwise in the same direction on both sets of Loop tracks. Now, the Loop is bidirectional, with right-hand running. This view is looking north with a southbound Ravenswood (today's Brown Line) train at left. (Richard Hofer photograph; David Stanley Collection.)

This is the north face of the CTA "L" station at State Street and Van Buren Street on September 13, 1959, looking largely unchanged since built in 1897. That year, the Chicago White Sox were in first place in the American League but had not yet clinched the pennant. The CTA was already encouraging baseball fans to take the "L" to Comiskey Park for the upcoming World Series, which the pale hose lost in six games to the Los Angeles Dodgers. The station closed in 1973 and was removed two years later. It was replaced by a station serving the new Harold Washington Library in 1997. (William C. Hoffman photograph.)

Six

LOST EQUIPMENT

From left to right, four generations of Chicago rapid transit cars are pictured in Forest Park on January 9, 1994—cars No. 6102, No. 1992 (formerly No. 2008), No. 1, and No. 4271. Car No. 1 was built in 1892 by Jackson and Sharp as an unpowered trailer for the South Side "L." It is now at the Chicago History Museum. No. 1992 was sold to the Illinois Railway Museum for parts. No. 4271 is part of the CTA's Heritage Fleet. No. 6102 was at the Fox River Trolley Museum for several years before being returned to the CTA in 2017. A 2600-series car is at right. (Bruce C. Nelson photograph.)

Cars No. 4318 and No. 2190 are shown running in express service along the Garfield Park "L." Steel cars and wooden cars were often combined in trains until the State Street Subway opened in 1943; at that point, all 455 steel cars were needed for the subway. Wooden cars were banned from the subway by local ordinance due to safety concerns. (Joe L. Diaz photograph.)

A pair of shiny new 5000s (Nos. 5001 and 5002) are on the Lake Street "L" bridge over the Chicago River in this c. 1947 photograph. These were experimental cars modeled after the Bluebird articulated cars built in 1939 and 1940 for the Brooklyn-Manhattan Transit Company. There were only four sets of these 5000s, which are not to be confused with the later 5000-series cars that CTA put into service starting in 2009.

The Met tracks ended at Laramie Avenue (5200 W.), and everything west of there was owned by the Chicago, Aurora & Elgin. When CA&E cut back service to Forest Park in 1953, the CTA purchased its fixed assets between DesPlaines and Laramie Avenues. Lockwood Yard, located a short distance west of Laramie Avenue, was once full of CA&E cars in midday storage. When Robert Selle took this photograph on November 6, 1954, the CTA was storing several old wooden "L" cars there prior to scrapping. Car No. 1113, at the front, was built as a trailer by Pullman in 1899 for the Northwestern "L." It may have last been used on Lake Street.

These 1000-series Northwestern "L" cars, built between 1899 to 1901, are shown ablaze at the Skokie Shops in the early 1950s. Air pollution was not taken seriously then.

These morning commuters are on a southbound CTA Evanston Express train in April 1970. The 4000-series cars used on Evanston were then nearing 50 years of age. They were state-of-the-art when built in the early 1920s—the finest rapid transit cars in the country. The first series of 4000s, built between 1913 and 1915, had more sideways seating. Their top speed was about 45 miles per hour.

CTA cars No. 6711–No. 6712, built by St. Louis Car Company in 1959, were part of the final order of 6000s. First introduced in 1950, the 6000s were all retired by 1992. This pair went to the Museum of Transportation in St. Louis but have since returned to the CTA. On October 1, 2019, they circled the Loop to celebrate the CTA's anniversary. Many riders looked around in amazement, as this was probably the first time they had been on these cars, which—for decades— were emblematic of the CTA. The top speed on these cars was 52 miles per hour.

The CTA tested new features during the 1950s, including high-speed motors and air-conditioning. The result was the Pullman-built 2000-series introduced in 1964, which became mainstays on the Lake Street "L," replacing cars that were about 50 years old. This photograph shows the interior of a 2000 around 1970. By 1993, all cars in this series had been retired, with none used in work car service.

After serving Chicago for many years, some of the original CTA "flat door" 6000s had a second life on Philadelphia's Norristown High Speed Line. Cars No. 6089–No. 6090 are pictured approaching Radnor on April 10, 1987.

Northwestern Elevated Railroad gate car No. 24 was built by Pullman in 1898. It was later renumbered to No. 1024 and converted to work service in 1955 as S-111. The Illinois Railway Museum purchased it in 1958 and has since restored it to its original appearance. This is how it looked on September 19, 2019.

Seven

LOST INTERURBANS

The Chicago, Aurora & Elgin interurban was built to a high standard and used third rail for nearly all of its trackage. Service began in 1902, and three years later, CA&E and the Metropolitan West Side "L" began running on one another's rails. This allowed the CA&E to run downtown to the Wells Street Terminal. In turn, the Met could now extend the Garfield Park "L" west of Laramie Avenue. In this view, an early CA&E train is shown crossing the DesPlaines River. Once Cook County and the State of Illinois decided to build an expressway here in 1945, this became a prime piece of real estate. The railroad refused to sell until 1957, when—perhaps not so coincidentally—the courts allowed the railroad to "temporarily" suspend passenger service. It never resumed.

The Chicago, Aurora & Elgin owned everything west of Laramie Avenue on the Met, including Lockwood Yard (5300 W.), which was used for midday car storage. In this June 1953 image, cars No. 28 and No. 207 are there. Both of these wooden cars were built by Niles Car & Manufacturing Company—No. 28 in 1902 and No. 207 in 1904. On October 1, 1953, the CTA purchased CA&E's fixed assets between Laramie and DesPlaines Avenues (areas where the CA&E no longer ran trains).

The interior of Chicago, Aurora & Elgin wooden car No. 301 is shown on August 8, 1954. It was built by Niles Car & Manufacturing Company in 1906 and modernized in December 1940. Since interurban trips were generally longer than those on the "L," more comfortable seats helped keep passengers happy. (Robert Selle photograph.)

On March 14, 1957, photographer Monty Powell captured this Chicago, Aurora & Elgin interurban train on a midday storage track at the DesPlaines Avenue terminal in Forest Park. Car No. 421, built in 1927 by the Cincinnati Car Company, is leading a five-car train. The wooden trestle used by CTA "L" trains to loop around is in the background. On July 3, 1957, the interurban abruptly quit passenger service in the middle of the day, stranding thousands of riders. Freight operations continued until 1959. Much of its former route became the Illinois Prairie Path.

CA&E cars No. 460 and No. 417 pause at Fifth Avenue in Maywood on March 6, 1958, during one of a handful of excursions run after passenger service was abandoned. This was as far east as trains could go at this point due to the construction of Interstate 290 by the DesPlaines River. Chicago, Aurora & Elgin tracks were relocated where they crossed the river, but the railroad was liquidated before any trains could run there. Car No. 460, built by St. Louis Car Company in 1945, is now at the Illinois Railway Museum.

By September 1959, the Chicago, Aurora & Elgin interurban line was no more. This image shows the Eleventh Avenue station in Maywood, looking southeast, while the tracks were still in place.

This is Chicago, Aurora & Elgin express freight car No. 5 (the second No. 5, built by Cincinnati Car Company in 1921). It is not often that individual employees can be identified in old pictures, but Clyde Goodrich (1887–1970), a longtime engineer on the interurban, is at left. His wife's name was Winifred (1882–1955). In 1920, Clyde lived in Aurora and was employed by the Chicago, Burlington & Quincy, a steam railroad. In the 1940 census, he lived in Wheaton and was employed as a CA&E engineer. The Goodriches are buried in Wheaton Cemetery.

When a railway is abandoned, the last train sent out retrieves stray freight cars and is known as a cleanup train. On June 17, 1959, Glen Brewer took pictures of the very last Chicago, Aurora & Elgin train as it passed through Villa Park at 11:45 a.m. Electric locomotives No. 2001 and No. 2002, built by General Electric in the early 1920s, are at the front. The image below shows the same location on June 12, 2020. The former CA&E station has been preserved as a local landmark, and the right-of-way is now the Illinois Prairie Path, the first rails-to-trails project in the country. The former Ovaltine plant in the rear was redeveloped as a residential property.

The Chicago North Shore & Milwaukee interurban, commonly called the North Shore Line, offered fast and convenient service between Chicago and Milwaukee up until its abandonment on January 21, 1963. It developed gradually, connecting smaller streetcar lines, and reached Chicago's Loop in 1919. By the late 1930s, it had a fleet of all-steel cars, and the company purchased two modern streamlined Electroliners in 1941. One of those Electroliners is pictured at the Milwaukee Terminal in 1949.

Car No. 37, shown at the Wilmette station, was built by the St. Louis Car Company in 1905 and was intended to be used mainly for city service. It was retired in 1923 and scrapped the following year. The interurban started out in Waukegan in 1895 and was incorporated three years later as the Chicago & Milwaukee Electric. By 1899, service had been extended south to Evanston, where riders could connect to Chicago-bound trains. Samuel Insull purchased the railroad in 1916 and reorganized it as the Chicago North Shore & Milwaukee. Insull also controlled the Chicago "L" system, and North Shore trains gained trackage rights into the city three years later.

Chicago North Shore & Milwaukee wooden car No. 300 is shown on an excursion trip in Waukegan around 1940. From 1939 until 1942, the North Shore Line allowed the Central Electric Railfans' Association to use No. 300 as its "club car." Here, it is parked in front of Immaculate Conception school. No. 300 was built by Jewett in 1909 as a main line coach. It was phased out of regular service in the 1930s and scrapped in 1947.

From 1919 to 1962, the North Shore Line's main Loop station and ticket office was at 223 South Wabash Avenue, adjacent to the CTA "L" station at Adams Street and Wabash Avenue and connected to the "L" platform via an enclosed walkway. After the North Shore Line's lease expired on June 30, 1962, the CTA provided temporary space for a ticket window inside its station for the last months that the interurban was running. (William Shapotkin Collection.)

North Shore Line car No. 413 (and a train) is shown turning north from street running on Greenleaf Avenue in Wilmette in the early 1950s image above. The North Shore Line abandoned the original Shore Line Route in 1955. East of here, the interurban joined the Evanston "L" at Linden Avenue. To the left of the photographer, the line ran north, parallel to the Chicago & North Western's commuter trains. The same location is pictured below in 2020. The storefronts across the street remain.

On September 9, 1952, this southbound North Shore Line train, running via the Shore Line Route, stopped at Foster Street in Evanston. Here and elsewhere, the North Shore Line had its own platform to prevent passengers from transferring to the "L" without paying another fare. It was not necessary to have a similar platform for northbound riders, as North Shore Line conductors would check tickets on the train.

North Shore Line car No. 255 is shown laying over on the middle storage track at the Roosevelt Road station on the Chicago "L." From 1949 to 1963, the North Shore Line had this station all to itself, as the CTA no longer used it, and trains from the South Side "L" went downtown via the subway. No. 255 was built by Jewett in 1917 and eventually converted to a baggage car. The Chicago Symphony Orchestra used it to move equipment to Ravinia. It was also used to haul sailors' baggage from Naval Station Great Lakes in North Chicago. (C. Edward Hedstrom Jr. photograph.)

In the early morning hours of a very cold January 21, 1963, motorman Bill Livings removed the headlight from the final North Shore Line interurban train after it reached Roosevelt Road in Chicago. This was truly the end of the line for the fabled interurban.

After the North Shore Line was abandoned in 1963, the Electroliners were purchased by the Philadelphia Suburban Transportation Company (also known as Red Arrow) for use on the 13-mile-long Norristown High Speed Line. The Liberty Liner "Valley Forge" is shown at Bryn Mawr in this September 1964 image. After the units were retired in the late 1970s, both units were saved, with one in Pennsylvania and the other in Illinois. The set shown here (No. 801 and No. 802) is undergoing a complete restoration at the Illinois Railway Museum. (Richard S. Short photograph.)

Eight

LOST TERMINALS

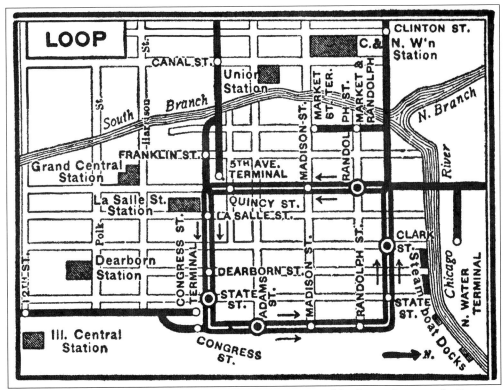

This 1917 Rand McNally map of the Loop shows the locations of the four stub terminals. Congress Terminal and the Market Street Stub predate the Union Loop. Congress was the smallest of the four and was considered inadequate even when it opened in 1892. Market Street was long enough to have two stations. The Union Station shown here predates the current one, which opened in 1925. In this context, as with the Loop, the word "Union" means it was used by more than one railroad.

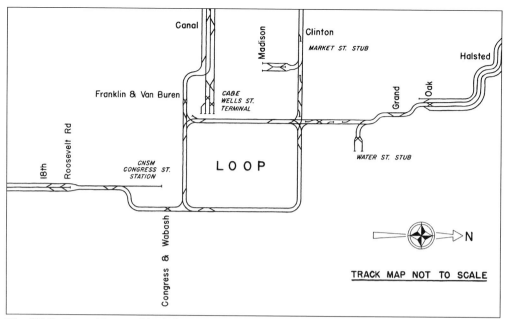

The Wells Street Terminal had the most complex track arrangement of the four stub terminals.

While the South Side "L" began under steam power, by 1897 inventor Frank Julian Sprague (1857–1934) helped transition it to electric power. In this April 16, 1898, photograph, Sprague is at the controls of car No. 139 on the Congress Terminal Stub, which was the original north end of the line before the Union Loop was built. At left is Harrison curve, which was built in 1896 along with the Wabash leg of the Loop. (Chicago Transit Authority Historical Collection.)

Congress Terminal was the original destination of the South Side "L." After the Union Loop opened in 1897, another station opened a short distance away at Congress Street and Wabash Avenue. Henceforth, the original terminal was called "Old Congress." Inbound service ceased in 1914, but a few outbound trains departed from here during weekday rush hours until August 1, 1949, the date of the CTA's major revision of north–south service. Shortly thereafter, the terminal portion overhanging Congress was removed for street widening related to the Congress Expressway. The North Shore Line continued to use the remaining portion for handling baggage until it was abandoned in 1963. (Eric Bronsky Collection.)

Four North Shore Line cars, including No. 254, are at shown at the Congress Stub in the early 1960s.

Congress Terminal's last use was for handling baggage and packages on the North Shore Line. Fifteen minutes before a train's scheduled departure from Roosevelt Road, one car (a combine) would be sent to pick up things before heading south to join the rest of the train. (John Horachek photograph.)

North Water Terminal branched off to the east of the main line of the Northwestern "L" north of the Chicago River. Kinzie station was here from 1900 until 1921. Merchandise Mart station, built on much the same site, opened in 1930. On September 26, 1944, this picture was taken looking south from the Merchandise Mart platform. The tracks at the end of the opposite platform went to the old stub terminal.

By December 1954, when William Robertson took this picture, no trains regularly served North Water Terminal. It closed on August 1, 1949—the date of the CTA's revamping of north–south service—but was occasionally used for car storage, emergencies, work equipment, and railfan trips. Here, a pair of North Shore trains, led by No. 157, is departing the terminal. (Eric Bronsky Collection.)

The North Shore Line became bankrupt during the Great Depression, but it eventually purchased two modern, streamlined, articulated high-speed trains dubbed Electroliners. One set is shown at the North Water Terminal on February 6, 1941, for a special inaugural trip.

In 1950, the North Shore Line modernized some of its fleet, dubbing them Silverliners. On May 17, 1950, the Silverliners were introduced at North Water Terminal. (William Robertson photograph; Eric Bronsky Collection.)

The first train of new CTA 6000s are shown on display at North Water Terminal on August 17, 1950. This was a convenient place to showcase a train without interfering with regular service.

The east entrance to North Water Terminal at Clark Street and Carroll Avenue is pictured in 1953. A poster advertises Harold Lang and Carol Bruce in the Broadway production of *Pal Joey*, then appearing at the Schubert Theatre. (Robert Selle photograph.)

This early view of Lake Street and Market Street shows where the Market Street Stub, which predated the Loop, branched off to the south. The Chicago & Oak Park Elevated Railway was extended east to Wabash Avenue in 1895.

The Market Street Stub is shown in this image looking south toward Randolph Street on August 14, 1925. It closed in April 1948. (Eric Bronsky Collection.)

The Market Street "L" terminal at Market and Madison Streets is pictured as it appeared in 1930. The "L" structure ended about 50 feet north of Madison Street. The large building is the Civic Opera House built by Samuel Insull in 1929. Market Street later became Wacker Drive. (Chicago Transit Authority Historical Collection.)

This is an early view of the Wells Street Terminal, which was used by Chicago, Aurora & Elgin trains starting in 1905. CA&E trains did not circle the Loop. Met "L" trains used the terminal during rush hours until 1951.

Pullman built the first all-steel Chicago, Aurora & Elgin cars in 1923. This picture was taken before 1926, when the Wells Street Terminal was renovated and expanded to add two more floors to the facade facing Wells Street. The terminal remained in use until 1953.

The Metropolitan "L's Fifth Avenue Terminal (later Wells Street) opened in 1904 and is seen here around 1913, just a short distance from the Loop "L." Starting in 1905, it was also used by Aurora, Elgin & Chicago (later Chicago, Aurora & Elgin) interurban trains, which did not go around the already congested Loop. In the mid-1920s, it received an attractive new facade with two additional levels by "L" staff architect Arthur U. Gerber. It closed in 1953. (*Chicago Daily News* collection, DN-0061194, Chicago History Museum.)

Chicago, Aurora & Elgin car No. 426 heads up a train at the Wells Street Terminal in 1944; it is flagged as an extra train (not on the schedule). This steel-bodied car was built by the Cincinnati Car Company in 1927. (Walter Broschart photograph.)

Construction of north–south Lower Wacker Drive began in 1949 and proceeded south at the rate of about one block per year. It was a major undertaking and a way to route traffic on and off the nearby Congress Expressway, then being built. By 1955, this project necessitated the rerouting of Garfield Park "L" trains, so the "L" along Market Street could be removed. The solution was to build a new Loop connection through the former Well Street Terminal, which had not been used since 1953. In these August 16, 1955, images looking south-southwest from the east side of the Quincy and Wells "L" platform, workers are removing the terminal's brick facade and laying tracks that ended up being used until 1958, when the Congress rapid transit line opened. Tower 22 replaced Tower 8 and controlled train movements. (Both, Robert Selle photographs.)

Chicago, Aurora & Elgin trains are shown leaving the Wells Street Terminal in July 1953, just a few months before the interurban cut back service to Forest Park. Car No. 46, built by Stephenson in 1903, heads a train of wooden cars. The tracks at right connected to the Loop "L" at Van Buren and Wells Streets. The large number "0" indicates what setting (0-4) to use for heat on the train. The photographer was standing in the tower that controlled the complex array of switches and the nearby bridges over the Chicago River. Met "L" cars terminated inside the building at right from 1895 to 1897.

This CTA electrical substation, located at 321 South Franklin Street, is an artifact of the old Metropolitan "L" and still powers the Loop. The tracks leading to the Wells Street Terminal went straight overhead until they were removed in August 1964.

Nine

Lost . . . and Found

Shirley Temple (1928–2014), then one of Hollywood's biggest stars, visited Chicago in June 1938, where she said the "L" looked like "trains on stilts." Here, veteran CRT motorman Charles R. Blade (1891–1983), a company favorite, demonstrates the controls of a 4000-series car during Temple's 40-mile tour on the "L." (Chicago Transit Authority Historical Collection.)

Chicago, Nov. 24th, 1896.

Mr. L. J. Southworth,

    Receiver, Plymouth Cycle Manufacturing Co.,

        Plymouth, Indiana.

Dear Sir:--

    On July 21st you wrote me in regard to the claim of this
Company against the Plymouth Cycle Company, for advertising, amounting to
$25.00, and advised me, at that time, that you were not able to state on
what basis settlement would be made, but would let me know as soon as
possible. Having heard nothing from you, I write to ascertain if you can
now give me the information.

             Yours truly,

                            Treasurer.

Advertising on the "L" was an important source of revenue, even in the 1890s. In 1896, the Met attempted to collect a debt from an Indiana bicycle manufacturer that had gone bankrupt. Bicycles were all the rage in the 1890s, and many such firms quickly came and went.

These seven weekly CRT passes, most worth $1.25, are dated between 1925 and 1941. "L" fares cost 10¢ during this entire period and were regulated by the Illinois Commerce Commission. After the CTA took over operating the "L," it could determine its own fares, and there were several fare increases between 1947 and 1957.

The throngs of people in this June 24, 1926, photograph were attending closing ceremonies of the Catholic Church's 28th International Eucharistic Congress in Mundelein, Illinois. Note the variety of railcars being used to move the masses to a temporary terminal on the North Shore Line's Libertyville–Mundelein branch. About 100 "L" cars were retrofitted with trolley poles for this event, and a loaded train arrived here every 40 seconds over an eight-hour period that day. At least 600,000 people were transported by rail to and from the event, which was the high-water mark for Chicago's transportation system up to that time.

Photographer Bruce C. Nelson captured this image of CTA cars No. 5173–No. 5174 at the Green Line Morgan Street station on May 4, 2018, decorated with Chicago's flag. This station, which opened in 2012, replaced one that was here from 1893 to 1948, returning the "L" to its roots as local transportation, since this stop is not served by buses and relies on walk-in traffic, as many original stations did. The "L" is forever in motion, always changing and adapting to serve this world-class, diverse city and looking to serve people now and in the future, as it has for more than 125 years. The "L" brings people together and takes them where they want to go. It is the "I Will" spirit of Chicago.

DISCOVER THOUSANDS OF LOCAL HISTORY BOOKS
FEATURING MILLIONS OF VINTAGE IMAGES

Arcadia Publishing, the leading local history publisher in the United States, is committed to making history accessible and meaningful through publishing books that celebrate and preserve the heritage of America's people and places.

Find more books like this at
www.arcadiapublishing.com

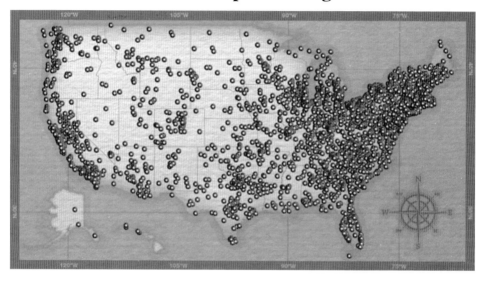

Search for your hometown history, your old stomping grounds, and even your favorite sports team.

Consistent with our mission to preserve history on a local level, this book was printed in South Carolina on American-made paper and manufactured entirely in the United States. Products carrying the accredited Forest Stewardship Council (FSC) label are printed on 100 percent FSC-certified paper.